*TO LIVE
LIKE A TREE
ALONE AND FREE
LIKE A FOREST
IN BROTHERHOOD*

Table of Contents

Preface	6
About Nâzım Hikmet	8
Eda: Intimations from Turkish Poetry - Murat Nemet-Nejat	10
Poetry Competition	
Selection Committee	26
Finalists:	28
Edwina Attlee	
Michael Beadle	
Kevin Boyle	
Alicia Brandewie	
Aaron Counts	
Ansel Elkins	
Terri Kirby Erickson	
Daniel Abdal-Hayy Moore	
Adnan Onart	
Glenis Redmond	
Maureen Sherbondy	
Honorable Mentions	97
Alisha Gard	
Maria Rouphail	
Dianne Timblin	

Preface

The Nâzım Hikmet Poetry Festival was organized with the aim of bringing poets, community, and scholars together in a festival celebrating poetry and honoring the Turkish poet, Nâzım Hikmet. As we look back over the third year of our work, we are humbled by the incredible heartfelt encouragement and support we have received from poets and friends. We would not be here without them. The festival has become a forum for cultural exchange and one that we hope that it will become a mainstay of the local and global cultural landscape.

The heart of the festival is the poetry competition open to all poets around the world. This year's selection committee consisted of Greg Dawes, Joe Donahue, Dorianne Laux, Jaki Shelton-Green, Hatice Örün Öztürk, and Jon Thompson. We are thankful to them for the conscientious and magnanimous job they performed. This year's competition received over 400 submissions. North Carolina poets submitted 53% of the poems. The rest of the poems came from other U.S. states (29%) and other countries (18%), including England, Canada, Greece, India and Turkey. Jon Thompson graciously volunteered to perform the first reading, which allowed the committee as a whole to focus on a reduced set of poems. The committee selected eleven finalists and awarded three honorable mentions. All fourteen poets are now permanent members of the Hikmet family and they are the strength of our festival. What makes us happy year after year is to find accomplished poets with previous awards and publications as well as rising poets winning their first poetry prizes. Four of this year's winners are from other US states. Edwina Atlee, from London, England became our second international finalist. The first international winner was Mel Kenne who had submitted from Istanbul, Turkey last year.

Last year's festival featured two successful additions to the program: A poetry workshop and the poetry spotlight, both of which were repeated in this year's program. Our instructor for the poetry workshop was Alice Osborne, an accomplished North Carolina poet. Alice showed the attendees how to use all senses in writing poetry. The featured poets of this year's festival were the world renowned poets Dorianne Laux and John Balaban. We are grateful to both for joining our festival to read their poetry.

All fourteen winners of the competition were invited to read their poems at the festival. Finalists who live far away and were unable to attend the Festival sent their videos, which the Festival guests watched on a large screen. Other poetry readings included Kane Smego of Sacrificial Poets, reading her own work; George Birell, reading Scottish poetry; and a number of the North Carolina Poetry Society's recent adult competitions winners,

The 2011 chapbook opens with a paper by Festival's invited speaker, Murat Nemet-Nejat, a poet and the leading translator of contemporary Turkish poetry to English. The title of his talk is Eda, Intimations from Turkish Poetry. As in earlier years, the rest of the chapbook is dedicated to poems submitted by the winners of the poetry competition.

We would like to thank Semih Poroy, the renowned Turkish cartoonist, for the use of his portrait of Nâzım Hikmet. Mr. Poroy is known internationally for his political cartoons, many commenting on current affairs and championing free speech.

This year's festival was made possible by a major grant from Turkish Cultural Foundation. We would like to extend our gratitude to TCF and especially to Ms. Güler Köknar, the executive director of the Turkish Cultural Foundation, for her continued support. The Town of Cary (Dept. of Parks, Recreation and Cultural Recourses) provided additional precious funding as well as the venue for the festival: Page Walker Arts & History center, a poetically beautiful place appropriate for a poetry festival. Special thanks go to Rob Garner, Kris Carmichael, and Theresa Dolan for all they have done. Thanks to the support provided by TCF and the Town of Cary, we are able to open our doors to general public free of charge and invite our guests. Last but not least, we would like to extend our gratitude to all our friends whose volunteer efforts made the festival and this chapbook possible.

April 2011

Buket Aydemir, Pelin Balı, Mehmet C. Öztürk, Birgül Tuzlalı
Third Annual Nâzım Hikmet Poetry Festival Organizing Committee

Nâzım Hikmet

Nâzım Hikmet, the foremost modern Turkish poet, was born in 1902 in Selânik. He grew up in Istanbul and was introduced to poetry early, publishing his first poems at the age of 17. He attended the Naval Academy but was discharged due to repeated bouts of pleurisy. Attracted by the Russian revolution and its promise of social justice, he crossed the border and made his way to Moscow and studied Political Science and Economics. He met the poet Vladimir Mayakovsky and other artists of the futurist movement and his style changed from Ottoman literary conventions to free verse.

He returned to Turkey in 1928 and spent five of the next ten years in prison on a variety of trumped-up charges due to his leftist views. During this time, he published nine books that revolutionized Turkish poetry and the Turkish language.

In 1938, he was arrested for supposedly inciting the Turkish armed forces to revolt. He was sentenced to 28 years in prison on the grounds that military cadets were reading his poems. While in prison, he composed some of his greatest poems as well as his epic masterpiece *Human Landscapes from My Country*. He wrote a total of 66,000 lines; according to his letters, 17,000 of those survived.

In 1949, an international committee including Pablo Picasso, Paul Robeson and Jean Paul Sartre was formed in Paris to campaign for his release. In 1950 he was awarded the World Peace Prize, which Pablo Neruda accepted on his behalf. The same year he went on an 18-day hunger strike despite a recent heart attack and was released under the general amnesty of the newly elected government. Following his release, there were repeated attempts to murder him. He was followed everywhere. When he was ordered to do his military service at the age of fifty, he fled the country and was stripped of Turkish citizenship. His citizenship was officially restored by the Turkish government fifty-eight years later on January 5, 2009.

Nâzım Hikmet did not live to see his later poems published in Turkish, although they were translated into more than forty languages during his lifetime. He died of a heart attack in 1963, at the age of sixty-one. During the fifteen years after his death, his eight volume "Collected Poems", plays, novels and letters were gradually published.

Many celebrations of Nazim's 100th birthday took place in 2002: the Turkish Ministry of Culture sponsored several events; UNESCO named 2002 "The Year of Nâzım Hikmet"; and the American Poetry Review put him on their cover and published a collection of his poems.

Eda: Intimations from Turkish Poetry

Murat Nemet-Nejat

In her address on Nâzım Hikmet that she gave at this conference in 2010, Prof. Mutlu Konuk wrote about Nâzım's poem "Straw-Blond":

> *Indeed, Nâzım's spatial location is split or doubled: he's both on the outside looking into the train and inside the train looking out. In temporal terms, the subject/ object is both in the past, gazing at the present, and in the present, gazing at the past. He is the spectator of his times —and his own time— from both termini. The train runs right through the speaker on these parallel tracks, which can only meet in optical illusions. The train here is a figure of the condition of exile— living on the go, in two time zones, and speaking their different languages. Set in an amorphous present, the poem is porous to the past and future, both on the scale of personal history and on the immediate scale of clock time (italics my own).*[1]

What Prof. Konuk does not say here is that this fusion of the objective and subjective, a sense of time where the past and present are unified into a continuous now, and both these experienced within a framework of exile —or longing— are not qualities peculiar only to one poem by Nâzım, "straw-blond," or to him as a whole; but define the very essence of the twentieth century Turkish poetry. Poets as different as Orhan Veli, Yahya Kemal, İlhan Berk, Ece Ayhan, Ahmet Güntan, Lâle Müldür, Sami Baydar, küçük İskender, just to name a few, each in his or her way explore and expand this matrix of linguistic, temporal and thematic relationship. As a result, they create a poetry which is stunning in its power and unique among the poetries of the twentieth century. In another occasion, I called the poetics creating this work Eda.[2]

Eda looks at the twentieth century Turkish poetry as a single poem—a hypertext—with inherent potentialities in which specific poems or poets constitute stations of a process which has its independent dynamic energy, its arc. Here is how I describe this process in "The Idea of a Book," my introduction to the Eda anthology:

> *While every effort has been made to create the individual music of each poem and poet, none can be really understood without responding to the movement running*

---

1 "The Forms of Exile,"*A Chapbook of Talks and Poetry, Second Annual Nâzım Hikmet Poetry Festival, pp. 17/8*
2 See *Eda: An Anthology of Contemporary Turkish Poetry*, edited by Murat Nemet-Nejat (Talisman House, 2004), p. 4/22

> *through them, through Turkish in the twentieth century. I call this essence Eda - each poet, poem being a specific case of Eda, unique stations in the progress of the Turkish soul, language.*
>
> ...
>
> *Istanbul is that milieu. Eda is the trajectory, poetics of a trip on a map. Sufism is its fusion of objectivity and subjectivity, a convergence of psychic time with history—a history of a city in twentieth century and of the soul of the folks passing through it.*[3]

In this address, I will discuss how Eda works, what its basic building blocks are and the kind of poetry it creates—the position of this poetry in the Turkish culture and at the beginning of the new millennium in general. I will end up by discussing a school of poetry, called the Poetry of Motion, created by a group of Turkish poets in the nineteen nineties, which reflects like an uncanny mirror the profound changes taking place both in Istanbul and beyond Turkey's borders.

I. Turkish

Turkish is an agglutinative language, that is to say, declensions occur inside the words as suffixes. This quality gives it total syntactical flexibility. Words in a sentence can be arranged in any permutable order, each sounding natural. The result is a language with a great capability for nuance. Here is how the phenomenon is described in *Eda*:

> *The underlying syntactical principle is not logic, but emphasis: a movement of the speaker's or writer's affections. Thinking, speaking in Turkish is a peculiarly visceral activity, a record of thought emerging. The nearer the word is to the verb in a sentence, which itself has no fixed place in the sentence, the more emphasis it has. This ability to stress or unstress—not sounds or syllables; Turkish is syllabically unaccented—but words (thought as value-infested proximity) gives Turkish a unique capability for nuance, for a peculiar kind of intuitive thought.*[4]

Language as process—"a record of thought emerging"—before it sets into analytic categories is what Turkish, particularly its poetry, contributes to the family of languages. This quality has three distinct consequences. First, the binary separation between the objective and subjective, so essential to English, disappears. Because thought in the process of emerging is both of the mind and stretches towards the world, the poem in this language acts as an uncanny mirror, reflecting an inner

---

3   *Eda, pp. 4/9*
4   *Eda, pp. 5/6*

reality and its reflection in an objective world. This core, basically a motion of language, is Eda. Second, because Eda records process as it is occurring, "emerging," events in Eda are in the present tense. Understanding this peculiar sense of time, the temporal space/zone in which Eda processes occur, is essential. It contains startlingly little of personal memory. The past is brought up and superimposed on the present, and the whole thing is experienced as a continuous now of the mind. The French philosopher Henri Bergson calls this "duration." A duration of the mind. Another French philosopher/critic Giles Deleuze calls it "time-image," a duration of the mind as eye movement. Third, the linguistic matrix of Eda creates, points to an abstract space, a there, an "it," which is separate from any individual psyche or biography. Interestingly, there is no defined distinction between "he," "she" and "it" and, due to the ambiguity of the Turkish syntax, references often bleed into each other. "It" is a space of physical desire or exile; but, simultaneously (and suddenly) of longing for union with "other," spiritual forces.

Here is a poem by the Turkish poet Orhan Veli:

Quantitative

I love beautiful women,
I also love working women;
But I love beautiful working women
More.[5]

These four lines are either a clever joke—a point of view a number of critics in Turkey share—or represent the ultimate poetry can reach, with no place in between. I belong to the latter group. Here objectivity—of a mathematical sort—is fused into an expression of desire. "More" is in a separate line by itself in the poem. This way "more" leaves behind its arithmetical, earthly identity of "wanting something more" and becomes a gesture, a vector towards an ideal union[, "not quite there." This gives the poem its enigmatic melancholy, its aura of exile.[6]

In the original, the line corresponding to the line "More" is "Daha çok severim."[7] Any inferior poet would have said "Çok daha severim," which would fit the logical development of the previous lines. By shifting the order of the two words—which its radically flexible syntax enables Turkish to do unobtrusively—the poem transforms a logical sequence into an act of desire, a gesture of spiritual longing.

---

5   *Eda, p. 67*
6   *Unless otherwise stated, all the translations are my own*
7   *The original Turkish version of "Quantitative" is: Quantitatif / / Güzel kadınları severim/ İşçi kadınları da severim. / Güzel işçi kadınları / Daha çok severim.*

The second is a poem by Yahya Kemal Beyatlı involving the Istanbul harbor:

That Summer

Was a summer reverie, summer, written by your desire
Each second, color, poem of satiation,
The garden still plethora, with your sweetest voice
If one day you long back oh for a station of that summer

Look at the nodding water of the harbor, you'll see,
That past night lying in its depth
The moon, large roses oh your most beautiful reflection,
In short, that summer reverie standing in its place.[8]

Though the poem starts in the past tense and seems to be about memory, almost immediately it turns into something else, the present, "The garden *still* (italics my own) plethora, with your sweetest voice." What the poem is saying is that the past needs to be transformed into a present, into a continuous seeing (and hearing), buried, embedded in the body of Istanbul: "Look at the nodding water of the harbor, you'll *see* (italics my own), / That past night lying in its depth / The moon, large roses oh your most beautiful reflection, / In short, that summer reverie standing in its place." In other words, there is no past; but a continuous present experienced as a tissue of seeing and hearing, reflected in the beautiful body of the city. I will talk about this beautiful body later. Suffice it to say, Istanbul here functions exactly like Hikmet's train in "Straw-blond": "In temporal terms, the subject/object is both in the past, gazing at the present, and in the present, gazing at the past."

The third is a poem by Celâl Sinay:

....
branch swings in the wind
let it swing in the wind
branch swings in the wind
will swing in the wind
branch swings in the wind
could branch swing in the wind
swings in the wind
was was swinging in the wind
branch swings in the wind

---

8   Eda, p. 32

> *must swing in the wind*
> *swings swings in the wind*
> *didn't branch swing in the wind*
> *branch swings in the wind*
> *let it swing in the wind*
> *branch couldn't swing in the wind*
> *branch swings in the wind*
> *branch swings in the wind*
> *wasn't swinging in the wind*
> *branch branch swings in the wind*
> *let let swing in the wind*
> *couldn't swing in the wind*[9]
>
> ....

Here, the invisible, the spiritual descends to visibility, as pure process—cadences, movements of a few words. This is the space at the heart of Eda, an ecstatic suffering, or bliss, experienced tangentially. The wind delineates itself on the visible leaves which the reader experiences reflectively through the senses. The sequence is similar to the movement of light in a camera obscura: absent object to film to eye/mind. The poem is a verbal photograph.

II. Istanbul

The processes of Eda in Turkish poetry are predominantly embedded in specific locations in Istanbul, creating a link between the city's history and the vector of the poetry. This relationship is described in some detail in the Eda anthology:

> *Here lies perhaps the crucial role of Istanbul in eda. Located on two continents, precious both to Christianity and Islam, with its endlessly contradictory nature, Istanbul becomes a site for a series of superimpositions.*
>
> *In the essay, "What children Say," Gilles Deleuze states: "... a milieu is made up of qualities, substances, powers, and events: the street, for example, with its material (paving stones), its noises (the cries of merchants), its animals (harnessed horses) or its dramas (a horse slips, a horse falls down, a horse is beaten...). The trajectory merges not only with the subjectivity of those who travel through a milieu, but also with the subjectivity of the milieu itself, insofar as it is reflected in those who travel*

---

9   *Eda, p.87*

through it."[10]

> *Istanbul is that milieu. Eda is the trajectory, poetics of a trip on a map.... its fusion of objectivity and subjectivity, a convergence of psychic time with history the history of a city in 20th century and of the soul of the folks passing though it.*[11]

Istanbul exists as an erotic (and political) body in Eda. Like the human body, it has its revealed and secret (or forbidden) places. The poems are often saturated with proper names, pointing to specific locations, creating a system of implicit codes, like a mirror reflecting the forces shaping the history and the soul of the city.

During the first two generations[12], the poetry is focused almost exclusively around water, the Bosphorus, the Istanbul Harbor and the old imperial city that lies on the southern side of the Golden Horn. In it, the city is a site/sight of stunning beauty of sounds, villas on the water, moonlight, mosques and other Ottoman buildings. This is the city for which Orhan Veli wrote "I Am Listening to Istanbul" and "The Galata Bridge," through which Yahya Kemal discovers the concept of time as a continuous present, for which Nâzım Hikmet yearns and from which he is exiled in his prison cell.

The poets of this period are all male. A considerable portion of the poetry is about love, almost all of it, illicit or not, heterosexual. The names of people filling the poems are Moslem, and the buildings referred to are Ottoman Islamic. Perhaps no single work embodies this vision of Istanbul better, in more concentrated form, than Ahmet Hamdi Tanpınar's novel *Huzur* (*A Mind at Peace*) which our colleague Erdağ Göknar translated magnificently. Two of its four protagonists cross the Bosphorus by row boat a multiple number of times. They listen regularly to classical Ottoman music, one of them constructing a utopian philosophical concept around one of its modes, *mahur*. He visits ancient Ottoman buildings around Kadıköy, on the Asian side of the city. A third protagonist visits the Grand Bazaar collecting antiques, the clap trap residues of a disappearing Ottoman life like a Turkish Walter Benjamin. The only character with a "foreign," non-Islamic name in the novel is a coarse, mercenary, divorced Romanian woman who seduces the husband of the female protagonist.

Despite its seemingly narrow focus, the poetry of these two generations repre-

---

10   Gilles Deleuze, Essays: Critical and Clinical, trans. Daniel W. Smith and Michael A. Greco (Minneapolis: U of Minnesota), p. 61
11   *Eda*, pp. 8/9
12   This is the period from 1921 to 1950. 1921 was the publication date of Ahmet Haşim's poem "O Belde" ("That Space"). 1950 was the year Orhan Veli died.

sents a very high point in Turkish literature. What is not named on the surface is entangled in the nuances, the mellifluous or awkward (depending on one's point of view) turns of its sinuous syntax, in its melancholy yearning tone, in its occasional references to "a child in underwear" playing by the water or a male's head "lying on a sailor's shoulder" or a fisherman with a Greek name, giving the seemingly transparent surface a dialectic opaqueness, a depth.

The future of Turkish poetry is implicit in the poetry of these first thirty years. One can say that it involves a liberation and unfolding of the forces submerged, like a sprung coil suppressed in the early poetry. Its potential trajectory is already there. One can sense it in the first few lines of Ahmet Haşim's "That Space" (O Belde"), the 1921 poem which starts the Eda anthology:

> *That Space*
>
> *Out of the sea*
> *this thin air blowing, let it play with your hair*
> *if you knew*
> *one who, with the pain of yearning, looked at the setting east,*
> *you too, with those eyes, that sadness are beautiful!*
> *Neither you*
> *nor I*
> *nor that evening gathered around your beauty*
> *nor that harbor from the sea,*
> *for painful thoughts,*
> *knows closely the generation unfamiliar*
> *with melancholy.*[13]
> *...*

The awkward, feminine lines, in melancholy winding around the harbor, constitute the essential music of Eda which in its original meaning in Turkish folk poetry meant the allure of the walk of a beautiful woman, "edalı güzel," "a woman *with eda*." Piercing through the macho, unitary facade of the culture of the time, the lines with eda first created by Ahmet Haşim—sinuous, arabesque, associated with women—run as a subversive and dynamic force.[14]

As a poetics, Eda establishes a connection between poetry and movements of the body—taking place in a space between the eye and the ear—pointing to an "it"

---

13   Eda, p. 24
14   Ahmet Haşim was considered "acemi" (inexpert in technique) by some of the critics. Obviously, they missed the power of his awkwardness.

which is a dance of the spirit.

III. The Second New

Orthodoxies IV

Pops out of a box, the beardless major-domo of harems, Köse Kahya, the comic hero of operettas. His skeleton out of the closet at last. Liveried, with golden threads. He haunts. A stuttering patriarch with a mincing slang.

He suckles a boy doll, its indigo fate of shame. How did it get stuck to him this wedding gift and the bride's golden threads in his hair all over the place? A silver hair pin. The play pay. Cheers.

(Ece Ayhan)[15]

The history of the *Second New*, the poetry movement from the early nineteen fifties to 1970, is too rich and complex to be discussed in detail within the scope of this address. In this poetry the focus shifts from the Bosphorus and the old city to the hills on the European side to the north of the Golden Horn, the districts called Galata and Pera. This area of steep hills and crooked, narrow streets was where the Levantine minority populations, the Greeks, Armenians and Jews, then lived. It also contained the entertainment and red light districts of the city. It was an area with theatres, bars, churches, synagogues, street hustlers, transvestite pick-up spots, etc.

The poetry of the *Second New* is full of Greek and Armenian names, names of transvestite singers or actors or historical figures who had to hide their sexuality, references to specific bars or churches, to words in Hebrew like Mitsrayim from the Old Testament, etc.

The *Second New* represents a huge expansion of consciousness in the range of Turkish poetry, erotically, historically and ethnically. Because of a plethoric, obsessive use of names, in the *Second New*, the reader often knows exactly where the poem is taking place, whether it is in the Bosphorus/old city or the Galata/Pera districts of the city. This creates a dialectic tension between the visible and hidden, the official and forbidden—the city turned into a fetish of the female body with visible, but mostly forbidden, parts.

---

15   *A Blind Cat Black and Orthodoxies*, trans. by Murat Nemet-Nejat (Sun and Moon Press, 1997), p. 39. This book will be reissued by Green Integer Press in 2011.

Fetishizing it, the *Second New* turns the city into a mirror, a photographic negative, in which the ethnic, political and sexual realities of its population can play themselves out. This movement is usually identified by its startling, often disjointed images. Though correct, this identification is deceptive. The power of this poetry lies elsewhere. Seemingly disjointed, images or references act as darts into wounds—or flashlights on suppressed fields. The thrill of a good *Second New* poem involves a sense of liberation, of expanded consciousness, experienced in a unique mixture of suffering and ecstasy:

Miss Kınar's Waters

She cried the smile of pebble stones with the raki from the carafe
from Miss Kınar now who became water to steep wells
with her straight hair what can she do in the theatre houses of Shehzadehbashi
she could not have enough hats

This bald Hassan, this baldie swept the darkness
his rebellious cigarette lit backwards to avoid any laughter
and a police enters fairy tales which go on ever since
parting the human eyelashes of children

And gathered inside her the sadness of the hands of an oud
playing woman, appeared suddenly into wells in the evenings crying
from Miss Kınar's waters.

(Ece Ayhan)[16]

Perhaps nothing expresses the dynamic and furious tension between the surface and the hidden more succinctly than a single word "orthodox" ("ortodoks") which as "orthodoxies" ("ortodoksluklar") constitutes the title of one of Ece Ayhan's books. The dictionary definition of "ortodoks" is "Orthodox Christian, holy, pious, virtuous." As slang "ortodox" means "whore, homosexual, pederast, betrayer, etc."[17]

Ece Ayhan's main focus is Galata and the secret sexual and political history of the Ottoman Empire. If he refers to Istanbul harbor, so much the focus of the previous generations, it is to boy hustlers frequenting its streets. His poem, *A Blind Cat*

---

16 *Eda*, p. 165
17 To read more about Ece Ayhan's use of language and narrative, see "Ece Ayhan Çağlar: An Afterword" (*A Blind Cat Black*). Among other things, the Afterword includes an analysis of the name "Kınar."

Black involves a trip of exile by a child across the sea to Jerusalem. But, instead of being a childhood fairy tale of adventure and wonder, it is a fairy's tale, involving his rape, which turns him into a hustler, kept by a pharaoh, "his arms tattooed with monsters."[18]

Cemal Süreya and İlhan Berk are two other central figures of the *Second New*. Süreya's focus in his first book *Üvercinka* (*Pigeon English*) is erotic love. In it the earlier poetry loses its "innocence." Eros becomes an experience of power, the thrill of seduction mixed with the potential agony of the inevitable loss. In Süreya, Turkish poetry reconnects itself with the sadomasochistic strain of *İlahis* (the Turkish folk spirituals). In this poetry, beauty is associated with death and violence. The resulting loss of the lover leads to a disintegration of the self. In ecstasy and suffering, often expressed in images of tears or other "flowing" images of water, the self longs for reintegration—for a greater union.[19] *The desiring self being in a state of disintegration, the speaker has no fixed point of view. It merges with the objects around it, creating a lyric with a elusive, shifting "I."* This gives Turkish poetry its abstract quality and originality. Transcending biography or personal psychology, poetry (self) turns into a process of spiritual motion.

What was suppressed and hinted at in Haşim's references to the characters Leila and Majnun,[20] in Hikmet's sense of exile and longing for Istanbul or a just society, in Veli's profound melancholy—what I call "a Godless Sufism" in another occasion[21]—reveals its total arc in Süreya's poetry, acts of fluid transformations from the physical towards the spiritual.

Having lived from 1918 to 2008, İlhan Berk's career covers three generations of Turkish poetry. He is usually associated with the *Second New*. His two fascinating books *Galata* and *Pera* give street by street, store by store descriptions (from pastry and perfumery shops to defunct whore houses) of major parts of these districtsç

---

18   *A Blind Cat Black*, p. 24
19   One can find examples of these processes in Pir Sultan Abdal's 16th century poem "The rough man entered the lover's garden "(*Eda*, 326/7) or Yunus Emre's 13th century poem "water mill why are you moaning" ("A 13th Century Dream," http://www.cipherjournal.com/html/contents.html)
20   Leila and Majnun are protagonists in *Leila and Majnun*, a poem written by the 16th century Azeri Turkish poet Fuzuli. In it, Majnun is denied his loved one Leila by her family. He goes insane and begins to wander in the wilderness, talking to animals. "Majnun" means the insane, the lost one in Persian. When her family takes pity on him and returns Leila to him, he says "You are not Leila," so transformed was she to a spiritual level in his mind through his suffering.
21   *Eda*, pp. 323/33. The name, the word "God" is perhaps the absolute no-no in Kemalism though all modern Turkish poetry reverberates with its suppressed, unnamed presence.

Like Ayhan's, his poetry is full of Levantine names. But, in one major way, his poetry is different from other *Second New* poets. The dimension of depth and discovery, so essential to Ayhan and Süreya, is replaced by horizontality. The pleasure of Berk's poetry is following the quicksilver movements of his mind transgressing intellectual, formal categories, assimilating and integrating the objects and concepts it comes across in sinuous, nuanced syntheses. In his poetry, language becomes movement and absolute process, possessing an abstract beauty. At its best, language relinquishes depth (relinquishing connotations), becoming light:

...

I SEE THE HOUSE AFTER I LEAVE THE GARDEN BEHIND.

To compare the garden and the house: the garden is wide open in the face of the close-mouthed, conservative quality the house characterizes (permeated with that despotism which wounded it long ago).

THE GARDEN DETESTS CALENDESTINE OPERATIONS.

Full of sound and voices.
Its face overflowing into the street.
Offering a female reading.

To compare them, it is sexual (what is not?)

THE HOUSE IS MORE AS IF TO DIE IN THAN TO LIVE IN.

Oh garden, the muddy singer of the street.

"Dirty Child."

Hello gardens, here I am!

("Garden," trans. by Önder Otçu)[22]

Berk's style is associated with the "long line," a twilight zone between poetry and prose—though very different from the prose poem—where the two morph fluidly in both directions into each other. In it, Berk explores and expands the possibilities of Turkish syntax as an agglutinative language where infinite desire merges with

---

22 *Eda, 100/101)*

infinite thought. The "long line" is the link between the feminine, longing sound of the previous poetry and what comes after the *Second New*. It is Berk's "long line" which a number of poets are inspired by and adopt in creating a new poetry in the 1990's.

IV. The Poetry of Motion

In the *Second New*, Istanbul is sliced in two ways. The Golden Horn divides the old city from Galata/Pera districts in its north on the European side (the two joined by the Galata Bridge); the Bosphorus divides the European side of the city from its Asian side in the east.[23] The poets of the first generation mainly focus on the old city, its Islamic history and the visual beauty of the Bosphorus. The *Second New* poets focus on Galata/Pera, its non-Islamic population and history and the underground life of the city. Both share the Istanbul harbor (the waters dividing the city cross-wise in general). In the first generation, water (the harbor, the Bosphorus) is associated with extreme beauty. Veli's "*I Am Listening to Istanbul*," and "The Galata Bridge," Beyatlı's "*That Summer*," Tanpınar's novel *A Mind At Peace* are quintessential, but not the only, examples of that. In the *Second New*, water and the harbor gain ominous overtones, as in Ayhan's *A Blind Cat Black* or Süreya's lyrics. They become sites suggesting death, seduction and rape. [24]

Up to the 1960's Istanbul was a city of about one million people. The old city, the Galata/Pera hills on the north, the shores on the Bosphorus, the Golden Horn and areas around Kadıköy on the Asian side represented almost the entire city. When the *Second New* poets pointed tangentially to specific places, revealing their secrets, the totality of the city as a single body was behind the images. That was what created the intimate connection the *Second New* had with the city, functioning as a mirror to its social, political and psycho-sexual life.

Starting in the late fifties, Istanbul began to undergo a profound transformation, expanding through the influx of the Anatolian population to find work. By 1990, it had turned into a megalopolis of twelve million —suburbs exploding in every

23   *The Bosphorus is a strait joining the Black Sea to the Sea of Marmara, and the Golden Horn is an inlet. They merge at the Istanbul harbor at an almost perpendicular angle to each other.*
24   *This classification should not be taken absolutely literally. Süreya's poem "The Apple"(Eda, pp. 144/5) refers to prostitutes "doing their business standing up" in the side streets around the train station at Sirkeci which is situated on the northern edge of the old city. The poet Necip Fazıl Kısakürek, who biographically belongs to the first generation, also refers to solitary hotel rooms around the same station. Kısakürek's poetry between the late twenties to early forties contains the subversive theme of a profane Islam, an inverted version of "Majnun in the wilderness. "Sirkeci is the locus of a slippage in the psychic map of Istanbul.*

direction— to which the previous demarcations were peripheral. The center had inadvertently moved. Nevertheless, though most of its best poetry had already been written by 1970, the stylistic influence of the *Second New* continued. The result is an excess of striking images with no physical actuality behind them which grounds them. This poetry has an element of phantasy, pointing to a place that exists no more. With rare exceptions, the images in it try a bit too hard to be striking, and its themes are personal and short of breath. It has none of the energy and the vision of spiritual longing of the earlier poetry and its Eda.

Almost instantaneously, this poetic crisis became resolved in a series of books published between 1991 and 1997, preceded by a crucial event that occurred outside Turkey, namely, the fall of the Soviet Empire. After the fall, Istanbul became an influx point, ideologically and economically, for the freed Turkic Republics in the East and the Eastern European satellite countries in the West. It became a point of fusion and movement. The poets in question responded to this transformation of Istanbul from a national city, with clear, well-defined demarcations, to a global metropolis. Though very different from each other, their poems have certain common characteristics. First, each involves the yoking together of at least two conflicting concepts. The poem becomes a field/site of synthesis. Second, a poetry built around images is replaced by a poetry based on movement. Often, in the cadences of long, sinuous lines—their music echoing Berk's "long line—potentially chaotic forces, concepts splitting away from each other move around each other weaving their synthesis. *The Poetry of Motion* reunites Eda with its origins. In it, what was a national poetry reflecting the history and soul of a city of one million opens itself up to a world beyond its borders, reflecting the central position of Istanbul in the new millennium. With it, Eda, the agglutinative music embedded in it, becomes an open-ended (almost abstract) medium, a tabula rasa, within which the conflicting, chaotic forces of the new global universe can dream its possibilities.[25]

I will end by quoting two passages. The first is from Lale Müldür's *Waking to Constantinople* in which she weaves a synthesis, projected into the future, between Istanbul's Byzantine (Christian) and Ottoman (Islamic) pasts. The second is from

---

25 *In my opinion, the pivotal works of the Poetry of Motion are: Enis Batur's "Passport" ("Pasaport") in Grey Divan (Gri Divan, 1990), Lale Müldür's "Waking to Constantinople" ("Konstantinopolis'e Uyanmak") in A Book of Series (Seriler Kitabi, 1991), Sami Baydar's lyric poems the first book of which is The Gentlemen of the World (Dünya Efendileri, 1987), Ahmet Güntan's Romeo and Romeo (Romeo ve Romeo, 1995), küçük Iskender's souljam (cangüncem, 1996) and Seyhan Erozçelik's Coffee Grinds (Telve) in Rosestrikes and Coffee Grinds (Gül ve Telve, 1997). The English translations of these works can be found in the Eda anthology. Further details on the Poetry of Motion can be found in the introduction to the Eda anthology (pp. 16/20) and in the essay "Turkey's Mysterious Motion and Turkish Poetry" (http://www.ziyalan.com/marmara/murat_nemet_nejat4.html)*

Seyhan Erözçelik's *Coffee Grinds*. This passage shows how the poet sees this new medium, reflected in the reading of coffee grinds, as an open ended field with infinite possibilities:

>   ...
>
>   *and then? then you are sleeping. you are sleeping inside Byzantium. first drops*
>   *falling from votive candles are burning your eyelids. a black tramp steamer*
>   *is waiting for you in sleep. a steamer as beautiful as black death. at the edge of*
>   *sleep.*
>   *if you wish from inside sleep cutting like a black wing you can reach*
>   *that steamer. but you don't want to do that. you now on the Golden Horn on the*
>   *water*
>   *are stretching one arm tied to a black steamer the other*
>   *to the well lit grief of the Tower of the Maiden.*[26] *you were going to be torn*
>   *into pieces if you hadn't woken up.*
>
>   *but this isn't the first of the Byzantium dreams with Lions.*
>   *nor the last gasp of a Byzantium of being torn and waking up.*
>   ...
>
>   *in the white washed and byzantine room one of the ancients is saying:*
>   *"here is a delightful balance: artist and human being*
>   *distinct and the same*
>   *both have gauged the depths*
>   *is that life is that beauty"*
>
>   *you are asleep now in the white washed byzantine room, you are very*
>   *alone. one of the ancients is saying, "Don't cry."*
>   *"Tomorrow is your birthday. Tomorrow a new name will be given to you."*[27]
>
>
>   *A mass of coffee grinds's flying to the sky. A profound sadness is getting up,*
>   *about to get up, and leave, leaving behind its space*
>   *empty, that is, nothing to interpret*
>   *in its stead. Either for good or evil.*

---

26   The Tower of the Maiden is located in the Istanbul harbor. It was inaccessible to the public until recently.
27   Eda, 212/6

A portion of universe waiting to be filled, is what's left.

Something has ended, you're relieved, have gotten rid of a burden. (What the load is, I can't tell.)[28]

---

28 *Rosestrikes and Coffee Grinds*, translated by Murat Nemet-Nejat (Talisman House, 2010), p. 14

"Poet, translator and essayist, **Murat Nemet-Nejat**'s edited and largely translated *Eda: An Anthology of Contemporary Turkish Poetry* (2004), translated *Orhan Veli, I*, Orhan Veli (1989), Ece Ayhan, *A Blind Cat Black and Orthodoxies* (1997), and Seyhan Erözçelik, *Rosestrikes and Coffee Grinds* (2010). He is the author of *The Peripheral Space of Photography* (2004) and, recently, the memoir/essay *Istanbul Noir* (2011), the poems *steps* (2008), *Prelude* (2009), *Disappearances* (2010) and *Alphabet Dialogue/Penis Monologues* (2010). His poem *The Structure of Escape* will be published by Talisman House in 2011. He is presently working on the long poem *The Structure of Escape*.

Poetry Competition Selection Committee
(*in alphabetical order*)

Greg Dawes
Greg Dawes is professor of Latin American Studies and Cultural Theory at North Carolina State University and editor of the peer reviewed electronic journal, *A Contracorriente*. His books include *Aesthetics and Revolution: Nicaraguan Poetry, 1979-1990*, *Verses Against the Darkness: Pablo Neruda's Poetry and Politics*, and *Poetas Ante La Modernidad: Las Ideas Esteticas y Politicas de Vallejo, Huidobro, Neruda y Paz*.

Joseph Donahue
Joseph Donahue is a poet and the author of *Before Creation*, *Monitions of the Approach*, *World Well Broken*, *Incidental Eclipse*, and most recently, *Terra Lucida*, an ongoing poetic sequence. Along with Leonard Schwartz and Edward Foster, he edited the anthology of contemporary poetry, *Primary Trouble*. With Edward Foster he edited a volume of essays, *The World in Space and Time, Towards a History of Innovative American Poetry 1970-2000*. He is a *senior Lecturing Fellow in the English department at Duke University*

Jaki Shelton Green
Jaki Shelton Green was selected as the first Piedmont Laureate in 2009. She is the 2003 recipient of the North Carolina Award for Literature and the 2007 Sam Ragan Award. In 2006 she was awarded a residency at The Taller Portobelo Artist Colony in historic Portobelo, Panama. She has received numerous other awards, including selections of her work choreographed and performed by the Chuck Davis African Dance Company at the Kennedy Center. Her publications (Carolina Wren Press) include *Dead on Arrival*, *Dead on Arrival and New Poems*, *Masks*, *Conjure Blues*, *singing a tree into dance*, *breath of the song*, and author of *Blue Opal*, a play. She is a creativity coach and arts and humanities program consultant throughout the U.S, Europe, the Caribbean Islands, Central and South America.

Dorianne Laux
Dorianne Laux's most recent collections are The Book of Men and Facts about the Moon. A finalist for the National Book Critics Circle Award, and winner of the Oregon Book Award, Laux is also author of Awake, What We Carry, and Smoke from BOA Editions, as well as a fine press edition, Dark Charms, from Red Dragonfly Press. She teaches poetry in the MFA Program at North Carolina State University and is founding faculty at Pacific University's Low Residency MFA Program.

Hatice Örün Öztürk

Hatice Örün Öztürk is a teaching associate professor in Electrical and Computer and Biomedical Engineering departments. Her poems were published by different magazines in Turkey. Recently, her translations of Mahmoud Darwish poems from Arabic to Turkish were published in Varlık.

Jon Thompson

Jon Thompson teaches at NCSU, where he edits the international, online journal *Free Verse: A Journal of Contemporary Poetry & Poetics* and the single-author poetry series, *Free Verse Editions*. His first collection, *The Book of the Floating World*, was reissued in 2007. His collection of lyrical essays, *After Paradise: Essays on the Fate of American Writing*, appeared in 2009. At present, he is working on a new collection of poems, tentatively entitled *American Landscapes*.

Poetry Selection Committee (from left to right): Jaki Shelton-Green, Dorianne Laux, Joe Donahue, Jon Thompson, Greg Dawes & Hatice Örün Öztürk

# *Finalists*

(In alphabetical order)

Edwina Attlee

Museum

I put my legs in the water
They hang like hams in the larder,
Cool and gargantuan.

In this heat
I am held suspended
Like a specimen in a jar
Or a bunch of yellow peppers.

You have put me on the shelf
And all I can hear
Is the sound of blood in my ears
As heavy as dumb bells.

Edwina Attlee

Valentine

Morning scores along the edges of the day
Like a tin opener on a can of sardines.

Your kiss on my lips is sweet with cider
And the sea-salt of sleep.

I am bevelled for you, parched.

With a line of question marks,
Shakily drawn with your morning hand of tremor
You rescue my whole world.

We walk together,

There is nothing but the artichoke stroke of your skin on mine.
The warmth of you is my
Eye, my smile, my sigh.
I am as happy as a tuna fish in brine,
drunk, cosy, packed flat, I am fine.

Edwina Attlee

Inside the Whale

The great dental scurf of your molars
trawls lichen and krill and moss.
I am used to the dough smell, the tired yeast,
the fragrant fart of seaweed fermenting,
the Diaspora of scales
flitting by my feet,
trying the edges in tired waves,
again and again and again.
They make sounds like breath,
And stir a memory of leaves.

I used to climb your teeth,
Go rock pooling in their
Rotten crevices,
Tread carefully about the yellowing edges,
Slip on green dredges of plaque.
I have no time for that now.

Ha-noi
Your name is for
Junk ships and the plunk
Of sinking pots
Into water
To out-pour
The overflow.

In the monsoon
cabbage leaves drift
like petticoat flotsam
against your knees.
Rotten fish flow

Edwina Attlee

through the streets.
The power cut
Leaves roads
Black and wet
The drains
Full of paper
And pulp.
We eat soft glass noodles
Limp by the light of
A halogen lamp,
Haunted by the
Call of the siren
And the rasp
Of the water-logged
Engine
Gargling through the water.

Ha-noi,
Soft sound plugged,
Garbled,
Pitched high,
Like the staccato rickets
Of geese
Honking
At the moon
Just as sensible
And slow moving
As Oriental porn.

An alphabet of fence posts,
Tallies,
Scores.
An alphabet of

Edwina Attlee

Pick up sticks,
Daft.

Ha-noi,
Your name is for
Whale guts,
Goat's blood
And rice wine,
The chew of the
White intestinal
Noodle,
The hum of
The cockroach
Numbed by diazepam,
Under feeble bulbs
As dark as the
Moon glow.
Ha-noi.

I sit inside you
At the heart of your lake
At the arch of your neck
In the dome of your throat
Basilica cupped
And ribbed in the
High reach of your diaphragm
That touches with gargantuan love
The Delphic breach of your pelvis.

And I do not know what to do.

Edwina Attlee

Ha-noi,
I am prey to the curious lunar
tug of your sleep patterns,
have forgotten day and night.
know only tides
spelt out by the starry phosphoresce
of shrimp
and sea horses.
And the tuba buzz of your snore.

In your sleep,
Your are one big wheezing harmonica
The great bulge of your B-flat stomach
Burps Yiddish protuberances,
Vov, Kof, Yud, Daled, Giml.
A phlegm ridden alphabet
Of whale parps.
And I dream of organ grinders,
Hot water bottles,
Tough rubber
And the London Underground.
Captain Mannering's marching band
Red faced, ready for a nap.

Ha-noi I miss the earth,
I cannot remember a time before motion.

Edwina Attlee

Edwina Attlee lives in London and is currently studying for a PhD with the London Consortium. She is writing about space and the city. She won the Alison Moorland Prize for Poetry from the University of Leeds and has had work published in Poetry & Audience and Trans Lit. She writes for Kicking Against the Pricks and Machine Paper and is always looking for work!

Michael Beadle

For the man who sleeps near Tahrir Square

No pillow, no blanket
for this exhausted Egyptian protester

who's taken shelter from the rain
in the wheel base of a stalled army tank.

Fully dressed in faded jeans and a sport coat
he's worn for days, he lies pharaoh-like:

arms folded, defiant even in sleep.
Any moment now the tired gears of the state

could lurch forward, grind his bones
through the streets of Cairo,

but the soldiers sent to quash
refuse to fight. Crowds gather to pose

for pictures sure to become souvenirs.
Up they climb aboard spraypainted vehicles

and take in the view you get
from atop a wall

before it's torn down.

Michael Beadle

David

One rock from the River Jordan,
hardened by a heavy sun.

He tosses it a few times,
lets it drop in his palm

as if to lessen its weight
before loading a borrowed slingshot.

The crowd leans toward
this chosen one called to slay.

Each side bangs its shields, raises
swords, screams the promise of victory.

Too many voices to hear his own.
Then Goliath appears,

his thick arms scarred by armies,
sword scabbed with rusty flesh.

The boy steps forward trembling,
fingers numb, heart a tambourine.

There can be no second shot,
only this one, guided by faith,

aimed at the giant's forehead,
a temple doomed to crack, spill

its ruby secrets. Two armies inhale
as a stone hisses through sandy air.

Michael Beadle

Leaving Baghdad

She changes clothes
three, four times a day,
another dress, another headscarf,
always getting ready
to go out with friends —
to the movies, to a party
that expects her arrival
any minute. She keeps
saying she'll leave
but never does.

In the light of a cracked mirror,
she darkens her lips,
shadows eyelids
with the faint hues of dusk,
jewels her wrists and neck,
the tender places
where kidnappers once
shackled her husband,
hung him from the ceiling
for eight hours
and beat him with a bat
until he begged them
to leave his body
where his family
could find it.

Michael Beadle

After they let him go,
he fixed a ladder
next to the kitchen window
in case he had to escape.

I must go, she says again,
staring into the shards of her reflection.
Yes, he replies. They are waiting.

Michael Beadle is poet, author and teaching artist living in Canton, N.C. His poems have been published in various journals and anthologies such as Kakalak, Pinesong and The New Southerner. He has published two chapbooks and produced a CD recording of original poems called Kaboom. In addition to touring North Carolina schools as a writer-in-residence, Michael is the author of three historical books on Haywood County, N.C., including Haywood County: Portrait of a Mountain Community, a co-authored bicentennial work that won the 2010 President's Award from the N.C. Society of Historians.

Kevin Boyle

Things I Knew I Loved And Didn't Know I Loved

    after Hikmet

I always knew I loved my penmanship, my push and pulls,
The Palmer Method, the slinky-long ovals to improve my muscle motion,
But I did not know I loved the blue smear, or red blush
On my left baby and ring fingers, how, from the side, they look like
Bony lips saying, I did not know I loved you so, my comrade.

I always knew I loved a drink in the late afternoon
Or early evening, or mid-afternoon, the sun past its apogee and prime,
The decline and fall of the empyreal disk a clear reminder
Of my dog's death, the cracked bricks of my house, the flagstone
Cracking up on the patio, and finally even my own crash and burn,
But I did not know how I would come to love what Truman
And Uncle Joe loved, that early morning shot of whiskey,
The phlegm chaser, the pain tonic, the cloud lifting through the clouds.

I suddenly thought of flowers, how I always knew only women and girls
Really loved flowers, their fragrance behind the ears, the women's skin
Akin to magnolia blossoms, the anthers like little boxing gloves
They'd wear when we fought, their pistils etymologically like pestles
They'd use in the kitchen to crush pills to poison ogres, but I never knew
I too loved flowers, even their little Burpee bags of seed
Enough for me some days, those colorful adverts for the real thing
I'd plant and water and lose interest in after a few days
Until there they were like soldiers you didn't know had bivouacked
On your own property, all wearing the bright colors of their regiments.

Kevin Boyle

I always knew I loved boats, even little dinghys, even Sunfish,
How strangers would yell, Landlubber, right to my face
And I would turn and show them my ship-in-a-bottle, my corked talisman,
My Boy Scout badge, and then I would push out from shore, an oar
At hand, and sail towards the island of Inisfree, a kind of weed-choked paradise,
But I never knew I loved torpedos and submarines, even U-boats and Das Boot,
Until I visited the maritime provinces and fell in love with a dead ringer
For Marika, she with the scent of almonds and walnuts in her hair
From her conditioner, and I with a deep yearning for her harbor and mark twain.

I have some questions for the gastroenterologist,
Did you always know you loved looking into the empty canals
Of Venice at night, not a soul present in the mist, your bark
Sailing past the Isles of Langerhans and the elbows and hooks
In the bowels of the city, to put it politely, or did you never know
The love of the miner's life, your light going deep into the mine,
Hoping not to find coal or a canary, and then right back out, slowly,
The journey and destination both important, no?

Windows appear before my eyes, I always knew I loved windows,
Maybe the wood as much as the glass, maybe the old pulleys
More than anything, their frayed rope kind of emblematic
Of how rope, after time, frays. But I never knew how much I loved
Windshields and windscreens, until I learned that in Spanish it's simply
Parabrisas, "for breezes," the way parasol is "for sun" and paraguas "for waters"
Is umbrella or bumbershoots. Sometimes I inhabit a harem and have too many loves
For who can choose between bumbershoots and parabrisas,
Both so labial, percussive, with long dark exotic hair.

Kevin Boyle

I always knew I loved knowing if I was in a train or not,
Or if I was on foot or in transit at all, that sense of purpose
That makes a purpose-driven life, how I loved that self-knowledge
About whether I was running from something or just sitting in the shade
Of a big building—twenty storeys of shadow—my arm inside
Marika's pocketbook, or maybe just my hand, searching for a pen
To capture a thought, but I didn't know I loved that feel
Of being inside a pocketbook, how it feels like a little diverse city
With its leather and plastic and metal and hidden zippers
I'd just let sing as I worked along the rows of teeth,
And by then I had forgotten my thought, but I always knew
I loved that journey along the slide fastener, the zip, the blessed tooth and nib.

Kevin Boyle

Two Sides of One Half

All my life I have lived
As Nâzım Hikmet suggested:
With great seriousness
Like a squirrel.
Madly burying chocolates
In my sock drawer
For later, which arrives
Before you know it.
Wearing coonskin hats
Because coons are kin
With fluffed out tails
I chase. Racing from store
To store as if before
The great storm to buy
This and that I fancy. Or fighting
With everyone I know,
Mad in pursuit,
Raising my voice into
A kind of squirrely shriek.
But my wise mentor asked,
What if the squirrels' poet
Said they should live
Like the humans,
With mixed emotions flying
From branch to branch
Of the ganglia and stem?
And so I resolved to live
Like a man in the New Year,
Full of doubt and indecision,
But couldn't finally commit
And lived as part man,

Kevin Boyle

Part squirrel, through March
And into April, until
I couldn't live with
The contradictions
And began to bellow
Like a bellows and bugle
Like an elk, my thinning hair
Standing up like those tails
Of squirrels you see
That have been denuded
By fright or war or science,
And I succumbed to the ravages
Of spring, surrounded on my deathbed
For a moment by my family
Who were living their lives
According to Hikmet—swiftly
Changing course, racing
To avoid the traffic of angels
Bringing me into wholeness,
The angels who were living
As part man, part God himself.

Kevin Boyle

Kevin Boyle's book, *A Home for Wayward Girls*, won the New Issues Poetry Prize and was published in 2005 and his chapbook, *The Lullaby of History*, won the Mary Belle Campbell Poetry Chapbook Prize and was published in 2002. His poems have appeared in *Alaska Quarterly*, *Antioch Review*, *Colorado Review*, *Denver Quarterly*, *Greensboro Review*, *The Michigan Quarterly Review*, *Natural Bridge*, *North American Review*, *Northwest Review*, *Poet Lore*, *Poetry East*, *storySouth* and *Virginia Quarterly Review*. Originally from Philadelphia, Kevin now lives in North Carolina and teaches at Elon University.

Photo by Tess Boyle

Alicia Brandewie

Heimat
        -after Eavan Boland

In my sophomore year of college
I set out
to learn my grandmother's language.
I had yet to find that

her tongue was already lost to me
in pictures and maps as I noted
foreign words with a sweet clatter
and known translation.

And when I came to the word Danube Swabian
I saw that language is pliable
and the lure of Oktoberfest—
where I had danced in the correct month as a child
because the Donauschwaben Volk ate and were merry—
came back.

Wie Geht's. Auf Wiedersehn. Nichts. Long gone
snatches that mean without interpretation. How
I remember where each of them lived,
one for each direction through the front door
and one for a card game
that was simple enough for all our minds.
I can hear her. I could say to her

we will be—we have been—
where meaning is not tethered to language. Is transcendent.
We were—we still are—relatives
of a river dialect. But it has been too long

Alicia Brandewie

>   to try absorbing whole books of descendant phrases,
>   to wedge too far open
>   this afternoon, rank with the memory
>   of three days smelling of sauerkraut,
>   when the sun shines on my timid questions
>   and choppy memories
>   and Mother unwinds the stories
>   that I never asked for.
>   Never thought I could know
>
>   All the dear titles
>   Mutti, Vati, Oma, Otta
>   as they stick in the American air,
>   echoing from the place we've been
>   and are going into
>   where words like Spätzle,
>   Goulash and the like—robust still
>   as they always will be—simmer
>   and are simmering with
>   delicious anticipation. To nourish.

Alicia Brandewie

Ekphrastic

I am drafting a poem but every metaphor is beaten
by my mother's hammer—twang of steel on gold,
teasing my concentration until it's planished flat.
While I am writing down a luminous image she appears:
could you come hold this bezel so I can stamp this ring?
Pinning down the gold circle, I listen to the ultrasonic
vibrate away the grit between settings and stones.
I wonder if the whirr of my grandmother's sewing
machine ever snagged Mother's sketching;
if the click of the feed dogs made her pencil skid
across the page; and as she erased the offensive squiggle:
could you come hold this pleat so I can hem this dress?

Alicia Brandewie

Cognition

Mutti, what I did not know then
I know now.

That Mutti means mommy.
You were too young to be called Grandmother,
and your daughters already called your mother Oma.

Sewing is hard, straight lines the hardest.
I salvage my blanket with a slightly squiggled trim,
marveling at the matching outfits you made for your two girls.

In order to cook fresh peas, I must shell them first.
The art of unzipping their thick coats is not easy:
I snap the ends, and with a gentle tension slowly pull them open.

Some women go crazy when their hormones evaporate.
The doctors thought maybe that is why it started,
but Vatti would not take you to the asylum.
You were not out of your mind you were trapped in it.

Alicia Brandewie

Alicia Brandewie was born and raised in Wyoming, Ohio. She is currently an undergraduate majoring in creative writing and minoring in anthropology at Emory University in Atlanta, Georgia. She plans to take some time off after graduation and then pursue her MFA in creative writing. These three poems are the beginning of her senior honors thesis.

Aaron F. Counts

Swimming with Sharks

> *for those lost in the middle passage,*
> *and those still struggling to survive it*

In the underbelly of this sleepless beast,
purple blood pools in rigored bodies
and buttocks too long laying idle.
Shackles rust in stagnant air and scurvied
fingertips bleed as they claw at keyless locks.
The world is inside out.

On deck, old friends taunt.
Sun's thorny rays betray hollowed eyes
with shards of piercing light.
Ocean sears flesh as water washes
bloody excrement from weary legs.
Music is now the hungry wail
of a neighbor's infant son.

> *At the savage captain's beck,*
> *Now like brutes they make us prance*
> *Smack the cat about the deck*
> *And in scorn they bid us dance*

Violin bow shrieks against nerves
and we shuffle on stranger's legs,
atrophied limbs lumbering clumsily
in rhythmless survival steps
unfamiliar as the monotonous line
where sea meets sky.
But still we dance.

Aaron F. Counts

While we do, those whose guts
knot like the knuckles of an old
man's gnarled fist hunch over,
doubled spines ignoring the insistent
cry of the accordion, the cracking
sha-clack of the captain's lash.
Even if they live to reach
land, they'll fetch no gold.

Some broken some bound,
bodies are heaved into the sea,
bobbing at the surface
before they sink into the sea
where hungry mouths await.

But sharks are smart creatures,
so even as frenzied jaws snap
and sinewy flesh sticks
between rows of incisors,
they are learning from their past,
teaching their offspring the comfort
of full bellies and the virtues of opportunity.

The sharks grow lungs and limbs, climb
aboard ships and pursue flesh onto land.
Refusing to wait for their next meal,
they learn to bid us dance themselves,
with hollow-mouthed promises of riches
and respect and freedom.

Aaron F. Counts

At the savage captain's beck,
Now like brutes they make us prance
Smack the cat about the deck
And in scorn they bid us dance

Today we dance survival steps
on the decks of square-sterned ships
called Sing Sing or San Quentin or MTV or NBA.
We've named those dances hip hop,
crip-walk, sacks full of cream
and tomahawk jams. Dances that still fetch
gold while we are shackled
to the ghosts that gold affords.

In the underbelly of these sleepless beasts,
purple blood pools in rigored bodies
and minds too long laying idle.
The iron in our blood rusts behind bars,
on street corners and in goals
we haven't learned to pursue.

The sharks shake our hands and smile.
And when they do, if you look carefully
into their mouths, you can still see
the sinewy flesh of your dreams.

* From the abolition poem, "The Sorrows of Yamba," author unknown, published in 1795 by Hannah More.

Aaron F. Counts

My Name
after John Minczeski

My name was coughed from the mouth of a volcano and floated
in a cloud of ash toward the sea. It became netted in the sails
of a three-masted schooner and was pulled by strange hands
into the ship's dark hold. Shackled in that darkness, my name twisted
in the puddles of sweat and shit of the strange-tongued names
held next to it. It called those names cousin.
From time to time, it was forced onto the ship's deck where it cringed
at the glare of a strange sun. Eventually, the ship lurched into port,
and my name stumbled into the purse of a don't-call-me-English-man.
He tightened his grip and laughed with a tobacco-stained sneer,
while my name jingled in his clutch like coins. It emerged wordless
in this man's home and found solace in the smile of his daughter,
who treated my name like a pet, feeding it milk-soaked bread and morsels
of bacon. With a soft voice, she read my name books in the shade
of a black gum tree. In their secrets, she became my name, too.
That's how I was born, making music in the emptiness,
with my name laughing in the face of the wind.

Aaron F. Counts

Museum of Flight

I

While trying to defy the laws that bind
man to earth, early inventors constructed
would-be flying machines, clumsy
birds built of wood and hope, then hurled
themselves off rooftops, praying

for a miracle. Each time they crashed, they'd
shut themselves inside the lab, tweak
their machines, then re-emerge, looking
for a higher precipice from which to jump.

If you fall from high enough, for a few short
moments, it feels like flying.

Aaron F. Counts

II.

The summer of my twelfth
year, my sky-high aspirations
were wings that could carry me
ten feet off the ground--high
enough to dunk a round ball
through an iron hoop and pretend

I was somebody for a few
minutes. My cousin and I stacked
anything we could drag onto our
backyard court: lawn furniture, overturned
shopping carts, or the rusted five-gallon
can that would eventually take

a four-inch bite out of my leg. The gash
split my tan skin wide open, exposing
milky flesh that slowly mottled red.
I limped the rest of the summer,
yearning to fall that way again—smiling,
arms wide, waiting for the crash.

Aaron F. Counts

III.

Dozing over the Pacific, the air
becomes violent, bucking the plane
and startling me awake. I float
a couple inches above my seat,
tethered like a parade balloon
by a too-loose seat belt. I want

to anchor myself in your eyes,
to reach out for the comfort
of your cool hand, but you're still
asleep, undisturbed, mouth falling
open the way it does when you're
deep in slumber. Your chest rises

with a sigh and I exhale in time
with your breath, noticing
for the first time a mole behind
your jaw. It is safe and beautiful,
as brown as earth.

Aaron F. Counts

Aaron Counts writes and teaches in schools, in jails and on street corners alike, intent on dispelling the myth that literature is created only in the academy. With influences ranging from Chuck D to Charles Dickens, he often tiptoes the line between spoken and written forms-at least until that line ceases to exist. An MFA candidate at the University of British Columbia, Aaron is the co-author of *Reclaiming Black Manhood* and is poet-in-residence with Seattle's Writers-in-the-Schoolsprogram.

Ansel Elkins

Prelude to a Season of Gunfire

i

In her gray apron the housemaid
lies, black hair richly spread
across cool blue tiled floor.
She dreams of a boy she's never seen—

a boy who is opening a cracked violin

case. Hidden within the violin
is a small red apple
wrapped in salvaged sheet music.
Is this my son? Has he returned?

ii

A fire erupts from within
the house's most interior room.
Outside the street is crowded with vendors;
no one hears the alarm ringing inside, its shrill

cry of yellow finches calling from a cage.

Ansel Elkins

iii

Two boys, one knife: each
cuts his opened palm. Bleeding
crimson rises from within
& they join hands as brothers.

When the seething city sweeps back her graying hair

wild ducks to take flight, fleeing
through the veil of black smoke,
the birds' brisk hearts burning,
hammering with wings that tear

toward a gift of bluing sky where the present begins anew.

Ansel Elkins

The Libation Bearers
    — ghazal for forgiveness

Strange fruit hangs from these burdened trees. Keep the children away.
The Furies are sleepless with hunger, they weep for a bowl of honey.

I stand over your mother's grave. I sing for her,
tell your secret, offer to satiate her anger with a bowl of honey.

They bury their dead in honey Herodotus wrote
of the Babylonians. If our dead be bitter, let's sweeten their souls with mead.

Dust and wind rip through the palms. Soldiers
spit in the sand, play cards and gamble for the last bowl of honey.

The priest hoped to save us all. He cut the throat of his beloved colt,
siphoned his pooling blood into a bowl of honey.

Blackout in our district's streets. My son falls asleep to a sonata of distant gunfire.
From the lion carcass Samson retrieved a heart of bees, divine bowl of honey.

The young set fire to their own city. They live in borrowed souls. Call home
your field of bees to settle once more on the bougainvillea.
    Land's open hand of honey.

Ansel Elkins

With broken fingernails I dig through the hollows of the tree's
trunk, unearth the wild bees, a deafening swarm to reclaim their bowl of honey.

At night in the dormitory a deaf girl reads Ovid's exiled odes. By the window
with her hands she asks the moon, that illumined bowl of honey.

In wartime a mother quiets her baby with honey on his lips. Dear sleepless sons:
hold your breath, dive deep into the well. Here, your grandfather's rifle,
        your bowl of honey.

Our children play at the ghost wall, make necklaces from discarded bullets. They find
dried blood on stones, a fruit peddler's overturned cart, his broken bowl of honey.

And to you, the living: sing prayers to your burning homeland. Your god
will forgive. Your rivers will return. The morning's newest song
        will be a call to prayer trembling in honey's blessed bowl.

Ansel Elkins

This Side of the Mountain

1865

The horses remembered the way
and at last we've arrived at the other side
of the mountain. Blood of other men
stained into our boot laces.
Only we three heading home.
I ride my Appaloosa Big Man, a long knife
scar across his mouth.
On a stolen sorrel mare
a man who doesn't speak rides alongside me.
I helped him dig his brother's grave.
Strapped atop the pannier he carries his youngest son, fallen
asleep against his father's back.

The sun suspended in the sky
is too heartless to set.
My hat's broad beaten brim
casts a long shadow before the horses' path.
Crows in the sky head north
toward burning fields.
Above us they float like black scarves in wind.

Coming down the mountain pass, a panorama:
smoke rises from the rough open
mountain, its remains
of char and rock and ash.
Stamping through the dust
of ground, the horses' hooves make vanishing
sounds that speak to this
slow and inevitable homecoming.
Big Man chews at his bit,
jangle of his silver bridle is all

Ansel Elkins

I've salvaged of music.
I try to recall
the mountain's native name,
but how can this place keep
calling itself a mountain?
It's now only the ghost of a mountain—
flayed, bald, blackened.
And we are not soldiers returning;
we are men descending
the face of a dead god.

Tomorrow when my horse dies
I'll leave him saddled.
                       When flies
congregate at his nostrils
I'll unearth the buried silver
bit from his mouth.
And when we reach the ruined town nested
in the valley below, the people will inform us
that we survived.
But I will continue alone, walking
until I reach a sprawling live oak.
I'll nail to its trunk
Big Man's bridle,
let the ghost of my horse
live on as a wind chime in the stirring wind.
Here beneath the giant tree's sweetening
music I will begin
to build my house from new lumber.

Ansel Elkins

Ansel Elkins is an Alabama native who now resides in North Carolina. She is a recent graduate of the MFA program in creative writing at the University of North Carolina-Greensboro. Poems appear or are forthcoming in *The 22*, *The American Scholar*, *Boston Review*, *Ninth Letter*, *Mississippi Review*, and *The Southern Review*. She is one of four winners of the 2011 "Discovery"/ *Boston Review* Poetry Prize.

Terri Kirby Erickson

Blind

A woman, newly blind, has watched the light
fade softly, making a sound like rain.

Once, colors were torrential—
shapes, a downpour. Now the patter of memory

is all she has left—faces of friends, words
on a page, falling

leaves, her own body—all gone from her sight,
all lost in the swirling

fog. She does not cry. Instead, she places her
hands each day, on the life

that she remembers—tender, adoring,
as if it is a lover, sleeping with her in the dark.

Terri Kirby Erickson

Battered

She stands in the hallway, holding a dog by the collar.
Her hair is wispy and thin, her teeth crooked. The dog
growls deep in its barreled chest; her frown lines
lengthen. She knows not to answer the door. Her husband
wouldn't like it. But nothing she does is right, so what
does it matter? Bruises bloom and fade. Days bleed
into weeks. She has no friends, no family—only a dog
that hates everyone, and photographs she keeps in a box
beneath the bed. There are snapshots of her parents, arms
looped around each other, herself as a child—serious,
brooding, perhaps sensing already, the life that she will live.
Now there is a stranger on the stoop, a man who might do
anything. She pictures angels lifting her soul to heaven,
wonders if they sing to you on the way up. She can
almost hear them as the door opens, feel the brush
of wings when she lets him in.

Terri Kirby Erickson

Nannie White

Nannie White cradled Clyde Willis
in her lap, crooned a song he was partial
to hearing, come bedtime. They tried to take
him from her, claiming it wasn't decent
to keep a corpse aboveground so long,
but she held on tight.

What a good boy he is—
always minding his mama, never pitching
a fit to get his own way. And Lord knows,
he was the prettiest baby she ever saw—
eyes bluer than birdfoot violets, cheeks red
as holly berries.

She could hear them milling around
on the front porch. *She's plum out of her mind*
with grief. Can't you do something with her, Sam?
They ought to know better than to ask him.
He's a smooth talker,
my Samuel,

but you can't talk a woman's child
out of her arms. *I won't give in to it*, she said,
pain sharp as a stick poking her heart.
If I do, I'll crumble like an old wasp nest,
leaving Clyde Willis
to wake up, alone.

Terri Kirby Erickson

North Carolina native **Terri Kirby Erickson** is the author of three collections of poetry, two of which were published by Press 53—*Telling Tales of Dusk* (2009), which reached #23 on the Poetry Foundation Contemporary Best Sellers list in 2010, and her latest book, *In the Palms of Angels* (April, 2011). Her poems have appeared in numerous literary journals, anthologies and other publications, including *The Christian Science Monitor*, JAMA, *Verse Daily*, *Hektoen International*, and the *North Carolina Literary Review*, and have been nominated for both the *Pushcart Prize* and the *Best of the Net* Award. Her awards include First Prize honors from the North Carolina Poetry Society, The Writers' Ink Guild and the Carteret Writers Award for Poetry. For more information about her work, please visit her website at: http://terrikirbyerickson.wordpress.com

Daniel Abdal-Hayy Moore

The Bullet

The bullet sped through the air
going nowhere

Aunt Martha was ironing
ironically enough

on a high balcony
in Barcelona

Larvae take a few hours or days
to mature and then

look out!

The clothes were neatly pressed in a pile
and then piled in a press

Time has a way of keeping still
for important events

Nothing greases silence better
than an important event

Time was winding down
and space was sharpening to a point

Travel from A to B is often sudden
and brutal

A direct consequence of a true
concatenation of events

Daniel Abdal-Hayy Moore

poising a conclusion on the
head of a pin

which punctures the silence
with a bang

heard round the world
from balcony to bridge to battleship to

bathysphere bobbing in the bath of life

The bullet sped forward and
didn't look back

With grim determination
it didn't know where it was going

Though where it landed was the
end of all knowledge itself

As many waves as crest on the open sea
or clouds in the scudding sky

or something whistling through the wind
to deliver destiny's personal blow

like a signed love letter dipped in scent
and sent through the perfume of the air

to a fair beloved

Though we don't know it each blow is a
love blow

Daniel Abdal-Hayy Moore

The children were playing on the terrace
hoops and jacks and hopscotch and Clue

The president was signing documents at his desk
flags of all nations furled and unfurled

behind him

Like a kiss it landed where it
needed to land

Sent from a serious hand

The young soldier in mid-sentence
put a period to his life sentence

Though he never finished his last sentence
sentenced to eternal transcendence

Aunt Martha ironed another shirt

he'd wear only once

on a balcony in Barcelona

On a hilltop overlooking the sea

On a day without clouds

Above the noisy city

Daniel Abdal-Hayy Moore

Hard Thud

Hard thud at the back of the stairs

Slap of a skiff against a pier

Tin cans falling off the fence

A chained dog howling all night

Late laboratories of people hunched over screens

Grasses growing silently in fields

Slip of clouds across and through each other

Early morning kitchen filled with sunlight

Mathematical formula writing itself out in the
mathematician's mind around midnight

Developments in a mineshaft deep in the earth

A glass vase falling to pieces in an undisturbed tomb

Actor's entrance stage right who
strides to the center of the stage and

sings his lines

Nurse fainting from fatigue and a
young doctor coming on duty in fresh scrubs

Daniel Abdal-Hayy Moore

Squeal of brakes around a mountain curve

Fresh and fragile rain falling on alpine housetops

Sheep huddling together at an angle on a hill

Landslide that covers a village in ten minutes

Gradual blackout of a solar eclipse

Things going on in another galaxy

A child playing in a sandbox by herself

First smile on the face of a newborn

Daniel Abdal-Hayy Moore

Before I Go

Before I go I'd like to recommend
the mile high door that

opens from the inside
the ocean voyage that

circulates around in our blood
and a visit and salutation to

all and every bird however plain or
tatty you can find for their

pleasure is flight and their
loyalty is the window they'd

like to fly through into eternity and
not stop until they get there

The days are both short and long
the seasons both come and go

The treasures of the eyes are nothing compared
to the treasures of the heart though

far less tangible or perhaps far more

since that which dazzles darkens
while that which glows warms

And an outreached hand to catch another
is the rope that climbs us out of this

Daniel Abdal-Hayy Moore

abyss into the bright fields of heaven

Before I go there are so many things I'd
like to recommend other than the

Grand Canyon itself which lies under the
sky a living metaphor of the

deathlessness of death and the utter
dryness of lush abundance

even as its tiny river seen below from

the topmost perspective cuts its
way to the soul

There's rain and its patter on any roof
there's walking among trees and overgrown paths

There's beloved faces coming toward us with their
cheeks and eyelashes and expressions no

words anywhere can adequately capture

I'd recommend the roar of lions and
stampedes of zebra if I could

the nose dive of whales and the
flight straight up of larks before they

loop to descend

Daniel Abdal-Hayy Moore

I'd recommend the endlessness that
forgoes the ending to this poem

so that recommendation continues
flowing long after it's done

long after I'm done
and my recommendations simply

ring by themselves among the large and
small bells of everything hung

everywhere for our delight
and the wisdom that comes from

hearing them more clearly each time they ring
blossoms into a sky made

golden by that silvery sound

Daniel Abdal-Hayy Moore

Born in 1940 in Oakland, California, **Daniel Abdal-Hayy Moore's** first book of poems, *Dawn Visions*, was published by Lawrence Ferlinghetti of City Lights Books, San Francisco, in 1964, and the second in 1972, *Burnt Heart / Ode to the War Dead*. He created and directed The Floating Lotus Magic Opera Company in Berkeley, California in the late 60s, and presented two major productions, *The Walls Are Running Blood*, and *Bliss Apocalypse*. He became a Sufi Muslim in 1970, performed the Hajj in 1972, and lived and traveled throughout Morocco, Spain, Algeria and Nigeria, landing in California and publishing *The Desert is the Only Way Out*, and *Chronicles of Akhira* in the early 80s (Zilzal Press). Residing in Philadelphia since 1990, in 1996 he published *The Ramadan Sonnets* (Jusoor/City Lights), and in 2002, *The Blind Beekeeper* (Jusoor/Syracuse University Press). He has been the major editor for a number of works, including *The Burdah* of Shaykh Busiri, translated by Shaykh Hamza Yusuf, and the poetry of Palestinian poet, Mahmoud Darwish, translated by Munir Akash. He is also widely published on the worldwide web: *The American Muslim, DeenPort*, and his own website and poetry blog: www.danielmoorepoetry.com, www.ecstaticxchange.wordpress.com, among others. He has been poetry editor for *Islamica Magazine*, and *Seasons Journal*, a new translation by Munir Akash of *State of Siege*, by Mahmoud Darwish, from Syracuse University Press, and *The Prayer of the Oppressed* of Imam Nasir al-Dar'i, translated by Hamza Yusuf. The Ecstatic Exchange Series is bringing out the extensive body of his works of poetry, of which he presently has thirty titles in print, as of April, 2011.

Adnan Adam Onart

Made in USA

> Brave sons of Turkey! The 8th Army owes it to your bravery and heroism that it has been saved from destruction.
> General Walton Harris Walker, December 1950

The day he joined the army,
my career as the striker of the team began,
and he, the *Hammer*, became the *Korean*.
A week later, we received a fancy,
pin up postcard from Seoul
wishing us luck with the coming championship.
Then nothing! Month after month nothing!

Many started to claim that he had fallen
while leading a Turkish platoon to safety
cutting through the Chinese lines.
A few even swore that they saw his name
in an obituary for the martyrs of Kunu-Ri,
the protectors of our ancestral glory.
Some suggested that he had lost both legs
stepping on a communist mine;
shell shocked, he was confined
to a mental hospital in Japan.

But my guts knew:
crazy or sane; limbs intact or completely gone,
he was back.
He was back and for whatever reason hiding
in his mother's *witch-house,*
at the end of the *Dusty School Street,*
next to the ruins of the old madrasah.

Adnan Adam Onart

When my legendary free kick
crashed one of their rear windows
at the second floor,
(was it our last school day or an early winter break?)
before we could even disperse in all directions
as we used to do under such circumstances,
not one, but two balls came back
from the belly of the dark room:
the first one was our *muddy bomb*, alright;
the second, brand new and shining, (a basketball!)
definitely American made.

Adnan Adam Onart

Communist Bandit

> 18 May 1944, 12am, Bahçesaray, Crimea
> For Bekir Osmanov

His picture had sprouted all over the town,
on the walls of the city hall,
at the entrance of the mosque,
even in the small coffee houses,
as if to celebrate the early summer
in all languages: in Russian, Tatar
and of course, German:
COMMUNIST BANDIT.
MOST WANTED!
His eyes wide open – astonished
at the listed reward.

His rescue of the three partisans
from a Gestapo prison in the North
in the middle of a snow storm,
had brought him the highest of his honors:
Partisan of the Patriotic War – First Class
and a bullet – a mother's prayer away from his spine.

Adnan Adam Onart

Only a year later,
when crammed into the cattle car
by the NKVD agents, next to me,
he immediately kissed my hand:
Don't worry, dede, he said.
They'll understand soon,
this is a terrible mistake.
As soon as they closed the door though,
he started to cry:
Nazi collaborator,
enemy of the proletariat, he sobbed.
How can I take that?

His medals were stripped away,
but the bullet next to his spine
stayed forever there.

Adnan Adam Onart

Bowls of Dust

First came the Men of the Cross,
killed our husbands, our brothers,
took away our sons.
Thus the strength of our villages disappeared.
A thousand thanks to God, the Merciful,
the Seljuk Sultans rescued the ones still alive;
but stole our mules, sheep and goats.
Thus our already sparse meat disappeared,
milk for the children,
yogurt for the sick,
cheese, our only joy,
from the belly of our loaves disappeared.
Then came the Sons of Genghis;
they plundered our orchards,
pillaged our farms, kitchens and cupboards.
Thus our red apples, green plums,
the most faithful: onion and garlic disappeared.
Barley, no more; rye, no more; wheat, no more.
The bottom of the bottom –
from the tables, our bread disappeared.
Then the Almighty stopped answering prayers,
even of the holiest among us.
The generous clouds from his majestic skies,
the life-giving rain from our world disappeared.
Only a wind, a punishing wind stayed behind.
Earth in our eyes, dirt in our mouths,
we buried our neighbors, parents, and children.
Nobody could sleep day or night.
Then one by one,
from their tombs, the dead disappeared.

Adnan Adam Onart

A first generation immigrant poet of Crimean Tatar descent, born and raised in Istanbul Turkey, **Adnan Adam Onart** lives now in Boston, MA. His Turkish poems have been published in different magazines: *Soyut*, *Yordam*, *Kardaş Edebiyatlar*, *Kırım* and *Dergah*. His work in English appeared in *The Boston Poet*, *Prairie Schooner*, *Colere Magazine*, *RedWheel Barrow*, *The Massachusetts Review* and as Wallpaper in *Poetry Motel*. *International Poetry Review* published his translation (together with Victor Howes) from Edip Cansever, a Turkish contemporary poet. His *dislocation* and *diaspora* poems have been collected in a volume together with Kenneth Rosen's *Cyprus' Bad Period*, as *The Passport You Asked For*. He earned the honorable mention of the 2007 New England Poetry Club *Erikan Mumford* Award. He is also the author of *TURKISH: A Dictionary of Delight*, edited by Roger Conover; ZKM, Karlsruhe, Second Printing, 2006 .

Glenis G. Redmond

What My Hand Say

For great-grandpa, Will Rogers
born in the 1800's

My hand say, pick, plow, push and pull,
'cause it learned to curl itself around every tool
of work. The muscles say, bend yourself like the sky,
coil yourself blue around both sun and moon.

Listen, my back be lit by both. My hand
got its own eyes and can pick a field of cotton
in its sleep. Don't mind the rough bumps-
the callused touch. I work this ground

like it was my religion and my hands
never stop praying. Some folk got a green thumb,
look at my crop and you'll testify my whole hand
be covered. I can make dead wood grow.

I listen to my hand, it say, Work.
My hand got its own speech. It don't stutter
it say, Work, Will. Though it comes to mostly nothin,
this nothin is what I be working for.

Glenis G. Redmond

Come harvest time I drive the horse
and buggy to town. Settle up.
This is where my hand loses its mind,
refuses to speak.

Dumb-struck like the white writing page.
The same hand fluent on the land,
don't have a thang to say around a pen.
The same fingers that can out work any man

wilts. What if I could turn my letters
like I turn the soil? What if I could
make more than my mark, a wavery X
that supposed to speak for me.

Glenis G. Redmond

On the Way to Grandma's Funeral

> The woods are dangerous
> -Little Red Riding Hood

You set a South Carolina record,
for footprints. 109 years is a long time

for anyone to walk down a road.
My memory of you is as soft

as the calico house dresses that you wore.
The day you left, a quiet in us got up

and went too. We felt the terror rip through us
just like those large x'd flags waved

their heated tongues on the way to Waterloo
to bury you. They said nothing.

They said everything. How you meted your days
in Upstate heat. Coaxed flowers

like your head, unbowed and unbossed.
Your red Canna Lilies flaming like your spirit,

Glenis G. Redmond

the tallest of tall; our limousine, a submarine
sailed along holding your only living child:

mama and her five. We did not talk of the four flags
that we floated by, but we counted them all.

I don't even know how the talk started,
of our top three desserts. Willie says:

1) sweet potato pie 2) sweet potato pie,
3) that would be more sweet potato pie.

we rode on this laughter that you would have loved,
joined in with hush yo mouth chile.

You'd be proud of how we turned our heads,
away from hate: fixed our minds on sweet thangs

that stirred you 39, 872 mornings
to lift from your bed, to rise.

Glenis G. Redmond

Crystal Clear

I could see if it wasn't for my thirst
for sugar, how I could set myself free
from the wreck of my pancreas
& its irrational habit of circulating the blood's fire
to blur my stance. It's on me, I know, to get clean.
Some blame mother's milk, where the tooth
learns longing, my ache flashes akashic
red, black & green Motherland need
or the bitter void of it. I tried kicking this crutch.

But, I always fall below the Mason Dixon line
laced with Magnolias & the smell
of cattle up wind. I always come up
short, empty or high on somebody's story,
about my story, plots that don't hold ground.
I want some truth to tide me over
not the crystal sweets that don't address
the deep hurt I keep trying to feed.

Glenis G. Redmond

Glenis Redmond is a native of Greenville, South Carolina, but lives in North Carolina amongst the Cherokee Mountains. She graduated from Erskine College and the MFA Program for Writers at Warren Wilson College. She is a Cave Canem Fellow and an NC Literary Fellowship Recipient from the North Carolina Arts Council and serves as a trustee on the NC Humanities Council. Her latest book of poetry is titled *Under the Sun*.

Photo by Daniel Perales

Maureen Sherbondy

Clinging

The male anole clings
by mouth and teeth
to my son's middle finger.

Clings to his finger
like sadness that will not
release its teeth.

Maureen Sherbondy

Unveiling

My father's tombstone is unveiled on Halloween
while I am miles away, unable to travel north
once again, though in my head I return there.

I wait at my house with lit Jack-o'-lantern
adorned porch steps, while somewhere
children gather their costumes and pillowcases.

Far away, my brothers stand on autumnal grass
as the rabbi recites his prayers,
then my sister-in-law reads a poem she wrote.

My mother sets a stone for me upon the grave.
I set out a candy bowl beside my father's photo
as I wait for trick-or-treaters to arrive.

I watch as darkness lowers its veil
and no one knocks upon my door, not even ghosts.

Maureen Sherbondy

Two-Dimensional

The wife stencils in a house
with her design of wants —
here a child, here a dog,
here a fenced yard.

A husband is drawn in too,
tall man holding a briefcase in one hand
a wine glass in the other.

There are computers, couches,
bookshelves. But when a hummingbird
flies into the penciled
house, all she has so carefully drawn
washes off the walls

Becomes sky and rain,
a puddle of muddy lead and paint.

Maureen Sherbondy

Maureen Sherbondy is an award-winning poet and fiction writer. Main Street Rag published her first book, *After the Fairy Tale*, in 2007. *Praying at Coffee Shops* was published in 2008. The collection won the 2009 Next Generation Indie Book Award (poetry category). Her short story collection, *The Slow Vanishing*, was released in 2009. *Weary Blues*, her third poetry collection, was released in 2010.

Honorable Mentions

(In alphabetical order)

Alisha J. Gard

Inishmore

Hours after landing on the island
we went to see the cliffs,
to peer over the drop-off of a thousand feet
into the bluegrey tumble of waters.
The field we found on cliff's-edge
was sunk into the landscape,
like a trough or a cradle,
or a chute into the sea.

There in swooning grasses, rock-guarded,
we stripped naked and ran, shouting,
bodies pale, sun-drunk on the edge of the world.
We stood tall over the lichens,
pounded our chests, and called to the surf.
Grabbing hands to swing around,
we were first man and woman,
bare and alive.

We made a pallet in the softest place,
and lay back, crushing tiny white flowers
beneath us, and stared into the sun.
We loved as we looked toward America;
you kept saying that spot
was the closest you'd been to home,
apart from how I'd brought it with me.

Alisha J. Gard

We rolled and roamed
until you worried about
the tear-shaped ticks in our clothes;
so as afternoon settled
we picked each other over.
We made one last echoing *halloo*
into the rocks below, and left
our passing imprint in the weeds.

Alisha J. Gard

Chance Encounters in the Garden of Lights

where the spider webs are missing their spiders,
and you're inclined to notice how
a loosed strand of draft-drawn silk
floats differently through space than, say,
dandelion plumes or leaves of oak,
which tend to drift and skitter, whereas
the spider silk ripples, ribbons, catches
on invisible hooks in the air.
The huff and wheeze of the breathless breeze.
No one looks for the spiders here
and they don't produce themselves.

Here in this garden, not by chance,
the trees are blots and smatters of ink
against a sky that hurts your eyes
in that it is bright and insistent,
and shoves at the shadows of these trees.
But in places near the touch of the land
the color's been sponged to a fade,
though one knows it wasn't always like that;
in places the blue grades to smoke and
it's dried out like the dyes on an old record sleeve.

Here it's possible to have chance encounters
with angels if you like. Garden angels,
and guardians. Hovering in wreathes of heat.
Cherubs whose stone pinfeathers are bent inward,
suggestive gestures toward stone-eyed faces.
The eyes are blank yet they are not blank,
as they know what happens and what will happen—
certain angels are this way.

Alisha J. Gard

It's possible that when no one sees,
the angels have their own encounters, lightly,
in spite of stone hands and lips—as though
such things have given anyone pause before.
These are androgynous angels,
with boxy breasts and shoulder-fused necks,
Hellenistically-robed and not praying.
Their wings are pinned on
and the ripples in their hair are courses for rain.

Paths of bricks in the courtyard labyrinths
are interrupted by rusted grates
circling anonymous, apologetic trees.
Veiled urns sit inexplicably on pedestals,
purposefully purposeless and elegantly curved.
The arcs of niches bow their marble underbellies.
Light is in the angels' eyes rolled back,
the filtered sun through tree fingers,
the shimmer and pulse of nonplussed wings.

Tree tangles, stone-harsh sky, guarded angels:
the continuation of light-disoriented delight.

Alisha J. Gard

Three Scapes

Amphigory

This is where the bodies are buried, he told me, as we walked among nude statues with no arms. The women had no hands with which to cup their bared breasts, and after so many years of immodesty, their eyes rolled in unconcern. The grass swayed and swooned away from our soft-shod feet. Pollen christened our uncombed heads. Later the rain would come to settle the tree grains, and the worms would drown in their narrow burrows; but at present, it was their androgynous brothers and sons dying, scorched and stiffened on a concrete wasteland. A yellow-dusted discus thrower heaved toward that field of dead, and I thought it wasn't fair that the worms couldn't carry out their business if they too were rotted. Nevertheless, I supposed, there would always be more children, a new generation to gnaw through the soil.

Sentinels

When mother and I went to town, we always kept an eye out for my doppelganger. A child, and a leggy sprawl, I trusted the intentions of strange voices nibbling at my ears. They wanted to help me—and who wouldn't want to bless a rose-cheeked child? At thrift stores, I would pass through rows of mothballed coats, past cracked leather shoes; at market old ladies offered me curled and salted pigskins. Once my mother bought a bed frame made mostly of rust and left it outside, so whoever materialized would sleep in it and disappear again. Only my other self was welcome. My own bed was hung with mirrors so I wouldn't forget who I was looking for, and I made a mantra of the names I thought the other might be called. Though I was young and had never seen a sitar, it was but one letter away from "star" so I knew it must be beautiful. Someday I would have and play my own, and my likeness would accompany me with a pair of silver spoons and limbs streaked with rust.

Alisha J. Gard

Mr. Ford

An old man sat carving wooden ducks. Once he had stuck his hand in my mouth and withdrawn a bloody tooth while my grandmother looked on. But now, between wood curls, he sat with fingers pinched as though twisting a waxy moustache. When he carved, he thought about how the ducks would not float upright, how their unfinished bottoms would freckle the ocean—if only he could get them there. In his deafness, he couldn't hear the shrieking teakettle that had boiled all the water to a torrent of steam, dampening the ceiling. He had taught me to clamp my hands over my ears to keep the music from getting out, although for him, the music was there all along and was good for dancing. Now he feared his ankles would snap. Flocks of wooden birds matched the walls word for word, and the old man in his wrinkled tie named them over and again.

Alisha J. Gard

Alisha Gard was born in Placerville, CA and grew up in Raleigh, NC. She is in her senior year as an undergraduate student at UNC Chapel Hill, majoring in English, minoring in French and Creative Writing, and studying German. When she graduates, she plans to teach English abroad. Alisha currently lives in Carrboro, NC.

Maria Garcia Rouphail

Winter Light

Shuttling back and forth
on a rusting ferry across the Florida Straits
between Key West and Guanabacoa,

two black haired sisters with shy eyes,
folded their hands on their laps,
felt the iodine sea lifting and dropping
until it slid them into the harbor.

Quiet girls barely out of adolescence,
each traveling alone
(or sometimes with their mother),
keeping womanly faith,
whether husbandless or hungry,
when one or the other birthed a squalling baby.

Now we conjure them, the almond-eyed ones
whose birth dates no one remembered
women destined for potters' fields
grandmothers who did not see our births.

We sit with gingham ghosts in a room
the color of Caribbean coral,
stir the traces of stories recited on
rickety front porches in another century:

> *Came down with tuberculosis—*
> *Got it from their father, poor things—*
> *that bastard who never gave his wife a moment's peace—*
> *Yes, and made his little daughters wipe his bloody spit—*

Maria Garcia Rouphail

But Clara the Younger
the one with lungs as thin as moth wings
went north before her sister.
Hers was the deeper affliction:
a handsome man
incapable of keeping a dollar or a promise.
He filled her belly with a son, then another,
then fled when the fever came and the bloody coughing.

Had you lived, *abuela*,
after your sister bundled you sweat soaked
and pregnant onto the ferry
taking you home to your island,
would your sons have grown restless,
forgetting you in their search for a father?
Would I be the one re-membering you
in the pale Capricorn light?

Maria Garcia Rouphail

Showings
(after Theodore Roethke)

Some gatherings make the blood run quick,
clouds like a cavalry
amassing on a ridge of sea froth,
wind opening a toothless mouth
sucking up houses on a black prairie,
a continent like a dagger
plunging into the side of another continent.
Mysteries abound. Consider
the high green surge of sea weed and silt,
the gray gash on the iron earth,
the shiver of roofs and bones.
What comes ashore in a convoy of shadows
escorts the heart into a room of awakenings.
We bend toward something. We don't know why.

Maria Garcia Rouphail

The Deep
(after Louise Bogan)

The phosphorescent salt pools
and the rock encrusted mouths of rivers
where what moves, moves
the undulant bodies of the sea
and what dies, dies
in the outflowing tide;

Where the deep
remembers the rising moon,
and waves draw
black curtains over the breasts of the earth
to cover her nakedness;

Where the rocks hiss
in their endless respiring;
where the tides dilate
over the forests in the sea
on their way to the continents—

Remember,
in the night of your seeing,
that more things dissolve
than rocks, shells, and salt.

Maria Garcia Rouphail

Maria Garcia Rouphail is on the faculty of the English Department at North Carolina State University, where she teaches in the World Literature Program. She has published poems in the *International Poetry Review* and *Pinesong* (North Carolina Poetry Society). She has two poems forthcoming in *Main Street Rag*.

Dianne Timblin

Walk

the hills bore us up
in the cool air of early

a russet mass
    fox or rabbit

the brown grass broke under our feet
    what was one more day

I have worked at it for months   five
red pillowcases   one girl standing by a fence

a still-warm spot in the brush
where the animal had lain

Dianne Timblin

When you get there

there won't be a big fuss.
This will be a relief. As if
you'd just gone to check
wash on the line and come back,
dogs crowding in ahead,
the screen door smacking.
Everyone will be there,
but again, this will be no
big deal. The one slicing cake
will remark on your earrings,
which will please you immensely.

Soon they will put you to work
and this will make you feel right
at home. They might ask you
to get ice for the cooler or look
in the pantry for extra napkins.
(Yes, you'll need napkins there, but
they launder themselves.)
Don't worry; this is your first day.
All the hard jobs will go to someone
else. You won't have to feed
the cobra or wash the cat.

Dianne Timblin

You'll be surprised how fast
the day goes, how soon someone
shows you to your room, how great it feels
to stretch out in the space you share
with the possum and the parakeet (they
sleep in the bed, but this too is
okay) and lie there, full of cake and ginger tea.
Look out the window, count the earths
in the sky below you, make a wish.
Go ahead—try to think of something
you need.

Dianne Timblin

Still life with turnstile

the tile	the alteration	the platform
the sunglasses	the red jacket	the whir
the blue sign	the ratchet	the screech
the brown bag	the delay	the one witness
the pay phone	the map	the silence
the *doors closing*	the fare	the blue line
	the penny	

Dianne Timblin

Dianne Timblin lives, writes, and edits in Durham, North Carolina. Her poetry has appeared in *Talisman*, *Phoebe*, *Rivendell*, *Fanzine*, and *Foursquare*, among others. Dianne is currently researching and writing about historical wildland fires in the American West. She works as an editor at Duke University Press.

A chapbook of talks and poetry

First Annual Nâzım Hikmet Poetry Festival

April 19, 2009 • Raleigh, NC

Contributors

Invited Talks

Nâzım Hikmet: Harbinger of Hope
Dr. Greg Dawes

Nâzım Hikmet and the Poetry of Confinement
Dr. Erdağ Göknar

Finalists of the Poetry Competition
Judy Light Ayyildiz
Katherine Barnes
Jeffery Beam
David Need
Pamela Richardson
Christopher Salerno
Tony Tost
Chris Vitiello

Honorable Mentions
Mimi Herman
Güney Acıpayamlı

Poetry Selection Committee
Katherine Stripling Byer
Greg Dawes
Joseph Donahue
Hatice Örün Öztürk
Jon Thompson

A chapbook of talks and poetry

2nd Annual NAZIM HIKMET POETRY FESTIVAL

April 18, 2010 • Cary, NC

Contributors

Invited Talks
Nâzım Hikmet: The Forms of Exile— *Dr. Mutlu Konuk Blasing*
Brown University

Poetry Competition Finalists
Kamal Ayyıldız
Mel Kenne C.P. Mangel
George McKim
Scott Rudd
Anya Russian
Celisa Steele
Garrison Somers
Carolyn Beard Whitlow
Loftin Wilson

Poetry Selection Committee
Katherine Stripling Byer
Greg Dawes
Joseph Donahue
Jaki Shelton-Green
Hatice Örün Öztürk

Made in the USA
Charleston, SC
09 April 2014